ANTIGONE

Sophocles

Prestwick House

LITERARY TOUCHSTONE CLASSICS

P.O. Box 658 Clayton, Delaware 19938 • www.prestwickhouse.com

Senior Editor: Paul Moliken

Editor: Elizabeth Osborne

Translator: J.E. Thomas

Cover Design: Chris Koniencki and Jen Mendoza

Prestwick House
LITERARY TOUCHSTONE CLASSICS™

P.O. Box 658 • Clayton, Delaware 19938
Tel: 1.800.932.4593
Fax: 1.888.718.9333
Web: www.prestwickhouse.com

Prestwick House Teaching Units™, Activity Packs™, and Response Journals™ are the perfect complement for these editions. To purchase teaching resources for this book, visit www.prestwickhouse.com/material

ISBN 978-1-58049-388-8

Contents

Notes

What is a literary classic and why are these classic works important to the world?

A literary classic is a work of the highest excellence that has something important to say about life and/or the human condition and says it with great artistry. A classic, through its enduring presence, has withstood the test of time and is not bound by time, place, or customs. It speaks to us today as forcefully as it spoke to people one hundred or more years ago, and as forcefully as it will speak to people of future generations. For this reason, a classic is said to have universality.

Antigone has been read and performed for so many years because it raises questions that are pertinent in every age: How much power should the government have? What responsibility does a person have to act in accordance with his or her conscience? And, can the answers to both of these questions coexist with one another?

Antigone also asks what we owe to our families. Complex relationships exist between Antigone and Ismene and between Creon and Haemon. Then, too, Antigone has a relationship with the dead brother she insists on burying; she feels that Ismene betrays this dead man.

Finally, it could be said that Antigone represents feeling, even intuition, while Ismene represents reason and caution. Seen in one light, Ismene is rational and Antigone is insane; on the other hand, Ismene is weak and Antigone is strong. Whether you support one sister or the other, you will find that this is a problem with no easy solution.

Reading Pointers for Sharper Insights

As you read *Antigone*, be aware of the following:

1. The conflict between civic responsibility and personal duty:

    • Creon focuses exclusively on civic responsibility. He believes
      that a citizen's commitment to his city comes before all else; as
      ruler, his duty to the city is especially sacred. He says,

      > "...my country is
      > safety itself, and only when she is upright
      > can our sailing find friends. With laws like these
      > I will make our city grow."

    In the interest of Thebes, therefore, he declares that Eteocles will
    be buried, while Polynices will be left unburied.

    • Antigone ignores civic responsibility and thinks only of the
      obligations to family sanctioned by traditional religion. She
      sees her duty to Polynices as a requirement of the gods. She
      breaks Creon's rule in the name of divine law, and even
      anticipates gaining the reputation of a "holy outlaw":

      > "…could my fame be more gloriously
      > established than by placing my brother
      > in a tomb?"

2. The difficulty of resolving this conflict:

    • Neither Creon nor Antigone is the hero of this play; both are
      inflexible, and both cause suffering by their stubbornness. Both,
      however, are noble characters driven by principle towards goals
      the Greek audience would recognize as morally good.

- Moreover, the character who advises compromise, Ismene, is no more heroic; in fact, she seems weak in comparison to her sister.

How does the conflict between two good characters with reasonable explanations for their actions make the plot more complicated than a play with a clear hero and villain?

Setting

Setting

The play begins in front of the palace of Thebes, exactly as in Sophocles' *Oedipus Rex*. The sons of Oedipus, Eteocles and Polynices, originally agreed to share their father's kingship over Thebes, but soon afterwards Eteocles claimed sole power and drove Polynices into exile. Polynices found sanctuary and support in the powerful city of Argos, so much so that the king of Argos betrothed his daughter to Polynices. After raising an Argive army which he led with six other famous heroes, Polynnices marched on Thebes. Each of the city's seven gates was attacked by one of the heroes who were slain by a Theban warrior, but Polynices and Eteocles, a Theban hero, fought and slew each other. On the morning the play opens, the Argive army has just left Theban territory; the city is filled with relief. Creon, brother of Oedipus' queen, has taken the kingship without controversy.

Dramatis Personae

DRAMATIS PERSONAE

ANTIGONE, *a young woman; daughter of Oedipus and Jocasta; betrothed to Haemon; niece of Creon; sister of Polynices, Eteocles, and Ismene*

ISMENE, *sister of Antigone*

CHORUS *of the old men of Thebes*

CREON, *king of Thebes; father of Haemon; uncle of Antigone and Ismene through his sister Jocasta, mother and wife of Oedipus*

GUARD *of the body of Polynices*

HAEMON, *son of Creon; betrothed to Antigone*

TIRESIAS, *blind prophet and priest of Apollo*

MESSENGER

EURYDICE, *wife of Creon*

2nd MESSENGER

Antigone

ANTIGONE

Enter ANTIGONE and ISMENE from the palace.

ANTIGONE:
    Ismene, my dear sister through common blood,
    do you know of any evil from Oedipus
    Zeus[1] will not perform on us who still live? [2]
    For I have seen nothing—nothing painful,
5   nothing mad or shameful or dishonorable—
    that is not among your or my sorrows.
    And now what do they say? The general[3]
    has just put an edict over the whole city.
    Have you heard it? Or have you avoided
10   learning how our friends suffer the fate of foes?

ISMENE:
    No word of friends, Antigone, either
    sweet or painful, has come to me since we
    two sisters were robbed of our two brothers,
    both dying the same day by doubled hand.
15   But since the army of the Argives
    departed last night, I've seen nothing else,
    either to cause me to rejoice or to weep.

[1] *king of the gods, often portrayed as the supreme arbiter of justice and destiny*

[2] *See "Mythological Background" (page 65) for the story of Oedipus.*

[3] *Creon*

13

ANTIGONE:

> I knew it! For this reason I brought you
> outside the gates, that you alone might hear.

ISMENE:

20   What? You seem to ponder something deeply.

ANTIGONE:

> Indeed! For of our two brothers, Creon
> gives honorable burial to one,
> but dishonors the other. They say that
> he hid Eteocles beneath the earth
25   with well-deserved pomp and circumstance,
> as one honored among the dead below;
> but the corpse of Polynices, who died
> so sadly, they say it has been declared
> to the citizens that no one may bury
30   or mourn him, but must see him unlamented,
> unburied, a sweet find for birds to feast upon. [4]
> Such things they say our good Creon decreed
> for you and me—for me, I say!
> And he is coming here to announce it
35   clearly to anyone who hasn't heard,
> for he considers it no small matter,
> but for the one who does any of it,
> the penalty is death by public stoning.
> There you have it, and soon you will show
40   how nobly you honor your noble birth.

ISMENE:

> But what more, my poor girl, in times like these,
> could I do that would not tangle the knot further?

ANTIGONE:

> Will you share in the labor and the deed?

ISMENE:

> What is the venture? Where have your thoughts
>   gone?

[4]See "The Importance of Burial in Greek Religion" (page 67) for information on Greek burial practices and the role of women in them.

ANTIGONE:

45   Will you lift the corpse with this very hand? [5]

ISMENE:

You want to bury him, although it's forbidden in the city!

ANTIGONE:

I'll bury my brother—your brother, too,
though you refuse! I'll not be found a traitor.

ISMENE:

Madwoman, even when Creon forbids it?

ANTIGONE:

50   He has no right to keep me from my own.

ISMENE:

No, no! Think, my sister, how our father
died hated and infamous from offenses
self-detected, smiting both his eyes with
his very own hands. His wife and mother—
55   both words at once!—took her life with twisted noose;
then, third, our two brothers in just one day
slew each other, poor wretches, achieving
a common doom at one another's hands.
And now the two of us, left all alone—
60   think how very horribly we will die
if we go against the king's decree and strength
outside the law. Rather, consider that we
were born women, proving we should not fight with
     men,
and that we are ruled by more powerful people
65   and must obey them, even in more painful things.
Therefore I ask forgiveness from those below,
as I am forced to in these matters, and yield
to those who walk with authority.
For to do excessive things is nonsense.

ANTIGONE:

70   I would not order you; and if you change your mind

[5] *Greek has many words that indicate pointing. At this point, Antigone would take Ismene's hand.*

now, I would not have you do it with me.
Be whatever you want, and I will bury him.
It seems fair to me to die doing it.
I will lie dear to him, with one dear to me,
75   a holy outlaw, since I must please those
below a longer time than people here,
for I shall lie there forever. You, though,
dishonor the gods' commands, if you wish.

ISMENE:
I do not dishonor them, but to do this
80   against the state—I have no strength for it.

ANTIGONE:
Use that excuse, if you like, but I indeed
will go and heap a tomb for my dearest brother.

ISMENE:
Alas, how I fear for you, daring girl!

ANTIGONE:
Don't worry for me; straighten out your own life.

ISMENE:
85   Then, at least, proclaim this deed to no one;
but keep it secret, and I shall do the same.

ANTIGONE:
Oh, denounce it! I will hate you the more
if you don't tell these things to everyone.

ISMENE:
You have a hot heart for chilling matters.

ANTIGONE:
90   But I know I'll please those I should please most.

ISMENE:
If you can—you want the impossible.

ANTIGONE:

Well, then, I shall stop whenever my strength fails.

ISMENE:

You should not start an impossible quest.

ANTIGONE:

If you say this, you will be hateful to me,

95   and the dead will hate you always–justly.
But let me and my foolish plans suffer
this terrible thing, for I shall succumb
to nothing so awful as a shameful death.

ISMENE:

Then go, if this seems best to you, but know that

100   your friends truly love you, however foolish.

> Exit ANTIGONE *off stage,* ISMENE *into the*
> *palace, after which the* CHORUS *marches*
> *onto the stage.*[6]

[6]*See* parodos in "The Chorus" (page 70)

CHORUS:

Str. 1

Ray of the sun,
fairest light of all those shining
on seven-gated Thebes,
at last you appeared,

105   O eyes of golden day,
coming over the streams of Dirce,[7]
you sent away the white-shielded warrior
from Argos, running from here,
with your piercing bridle.

[7]*one of the most famous landmarks of Thebes*

110   He set forth against our land
because of the contentious claims of Polynices,
like a sharply crying
eagle flying into our land,
covered with a wing white as snow,

115   descending with many shields
and crested with horse-hair.

Ant. 1

He perched on the roof,
gaping wide with bloody spears
around our seven gates,
120 but then he went away,
before his jaws were filled with our blood
or Hephaestus'[8] torches could take
our crown of towers.
Such a clash of Ares[9] swelled behind him,
125 a hard conquest for the dragon's rival. [10]

For Zeus hates excessively
the boasts of a great tongue, and looking on them
coming in rapid flow,
over-confident in clanging gold, he threw down
130 the one rushing with brandished fire
to the top of his goal,
seeking already to proclaim his victory.

Str. 2

He fell in an arc to the hard ground,
torch in hand, the one who with raging onslaught
135 furiously was breathing
with the rush of the most hateful winds.
But, those things went otherwise,
and great Ares sent them to
various fates, smiting them,
140 with our chariot's strongest horse.[11]

Seven captains at our seven gates,
marshaled against equal foes, left
to Zeus the router bronze weapons,[12]
except those two wretches, who were
145 born of the same father and the same mother,
standing against each other with doubly slaying
        spears,
they both took an equal share of their common death.

Ant. 2

But since great-named Victory came,
rejoicing in answer with Thebes of many chariots,
150 let us enjoy oblivion

[8]*the god of fire, often used as a metonymy for fire itself*

[9]*The name of the god of war, Ares, was ofter used by itself to suggest the irrational aspects of war.*

[10]*Legend said that Thebes was founded when Cadmus sowed a field with the teeth of a dragon, out of which sprang the citizens of Thebes.*

[11]*Chariot racers in the ancient world always placed the strongest, fastest horse on the right end.*

[12]*The victor in combat often dedicated the spoils of his victory, usually his opponent's armor, to a god in gratitude for the victory. "Zeus the router" would be a common choice for this dedication.*

of the recent wars
and let us go to all the temples
of the gods to dance through the
night, and may Bacchus,[13] who
155   has made Thebes shake, be our leader.
Enter CREON *from the palace.*
But here is the king of this land,
Creon, son of Menoeceus, our new leader
in this new situation given by the gods.
What plan does he hold
160   that he proposed this gathered
council of old men,
summoning us by proclamation?

CREON:
Gentlemen, the gods have set right again
our city's affairs, after shaking them
165   in a storm, and I have summoned you here
out of all the citizens, knowing well
how you always revered the power of
Laius' throne; then, both when Oedipus saved
the city and when he fell, you stood in
170   consistent support of their children.[14]
And so, since in the same day they both fell
by twofold fate, each striking and spreading
fratricidal pollution, now I hold
sole power and the throne, because I am
175   the closest relative of the fallen.
It is impossible to know the soul,
the mind, and character of any man,
until he has proven himself in the law.
For if someone rules an entire city
180   and does not take hold of the best counsels,
but holds his tongue out of fear, I think him
to be the worst of men, now and always;
and the man who considers more important
than his fatherland his friend, I think him
185   worthless. For—and may all-seeing Zeus
be my witness—I would never be silent
if I saw madness creeping among

[13]*the god of wine and intoxication; son of Zeus and a mortal prince of Thebes, hence his close association with Thebes; also known as Dionysus*

[14]*Laius was Oedipus' father. See "Mythological Background" (page 65) for more information. "Their children" refers to Eteocles and Polynices.*

the citizens in place of salvation,
nor would I consider an enemy
190   of my country a friend to myself,
recognizing this: that my country is
safety itself, and only when she is upright
can our sailing find friends. With laws like these
I will make our city grow. Therefore, I
195   have made a decree to the citizens
concerning the sons of Oedipus:
Eteocles, who fell fighting for this city,
who earned every prize of valor,
will be buried and receive all honors
200   that go to the best of the dead below.
His erstwhile kinsman, however, I mean
Polynices, who returned from exile
with hopes of burning his native land and
ancestral gods from top to bottom,
205   wishing to feast on kindred blood and lead
the rest into slavery, it has been
decreed that in this city he shall be
neither buried nor mourned by anyone,
but everyone must leave him unburied,
210   a feast for birds and dogs, an outrage to see.
This is my judgment, and never from me
will the base take equal honor to the good;
but whoever is friendly to this city will
in life and death be equally honored by me.

CHORUS:
215   You are at your pleasure to decide this,
son of Menoeceus, concerning the city's
friend and foe. You may use any habit both
with the dead and with all of us who live.

CREON:
Then I would have you keep watch over my words.

CHORUS:
Give this task to a younger man to do.

CREON:

220   No, the corpse's guards are already posted.

CHORUS:

        What would you have us do beyond this?

CREON:

        Do not join with those disobeying it.

CHORUS:

        No man is so foolish as to lust for death.

CREON:

        And truly that is this deed's reward, but
225   often profit has destroyed men through their hopes.

Enter GUARD from offstage.

GUARD:

        My lord, I will not say that I come breathless
        from rushing or quickly moving my feet,
        for often my thoughts stopped me in my place,
        and I'd wheel around on the road back where I came.
230   My heart kept talking to me, telling me,
        "Poor fool, why are you going where you're sure
        to be punished?" "Idiot, you stopping
        again? If Creon hears it from someone else,
        then you'll really pay for it!" Twisting like this
235   I made my way, the opposite of haste,
        and thus a short road became a long one.
        But, at last, the vote for coming won the day.
        Even if I have nothing to say, I'll tell you
        anyway, for I came seized by one hope,
240   to suffer nothing but my fated doom.

CREON:

        Why is it you have this lack of spirit?

GUARD:

        I wish to tell you first my side of it,

for I neither did the deed nor saw him
who did, nor do I deserve any harm.

CREON:

245   You're really trying to talk around the problem.
Clearly you have something new to report.

GUARD:

Terrible things make a man hesitate.

CREON:

Then why don't you speak and go away free?

GUARD:

And I'm saying it! Just now someone has
250   buried the corpse and gone off, sprinkling dust
over its flesh and performing the due rites.[15]

CREON:

What did you say? What man has dared to do this?

GUARD:

I don't know, for there was no stroke of a
mattock or heap from a shovel, just hard
255   earth and dry land, unbroken, no trace
of wheels, but the workman worked without sign.
When the day watch first showed it to us, we
all thought it a most distressing marvel.
For, although he was hidden from sight,
260   he wasn't entombed *per se*, but there was
a little dust on him, as from one fleeing
a curse.[16] Yet there weren't any signs of beasts
or a dog coming near him, nor did the body
seem mangled. Evil words broke out among us,
265   guard accusing guard, and it would have come
to blows in the end, for there was no one
to stop us. Every single man stood
on trial, but none could be convicted,
everyone claimed he knew nothing.
270   We were ready even for trial by ordeal,

[15]*Sprinkling dust over the body was the crucial step to bring the spirit peace.*

[16]*Anyone passing an unburied corpse who did not throw some dust over it would come under a curse from the ghost of the corpse.*

to walk through fire, to swear to the gods
that we had neither done the deed nor been
privy to the planning or the doing.
At last, when our investigation came
275   to nothing, one man spoke up, who caused us
all to nod our heads to the ground in fear,
for we had no alternative to what
he said or a safe course for ourselves
if we obeyed. His idea was that
280   this deed must be brought to you and not concealed.
This idea prevailed, and the lot chose
unhappy me to take this good office.
So here I am, unwilling—I know well—
among the unwilling, for no one
285   cherishes the messenger of evil words.

CHORUS:

My lord, my mind has long been counseling
that perhaps this was the work of the gods.

CREON:

Stop, before you say something to really
anger me and show yourself both old and foolish!
290   You speak insufferably when you claim
the gods have some concern for this carcass.
Would they honor him as a benefactor
and bury him, who came to set fire to
their temples girt with columns, to scatter
295   their donations, earth, and laws? Or do you
revere gods who honor evil men?
It isn't so. Rather, even before,
men in the city resisted this decree
and mumbled against me secretly,
300   shaking their heads and refusing to bear
the yoke as they should, to gratify me.
These guards here have been bribed—I can see that
clearly—by such men to do this, for no
institution has so harmed humanity
305   as the creation of money. It's destroyed
even cities, it has expelled men from

their homes; it teaches the minds of honest
men to deviate and take up foul things.
It has shown men how to be villainous
310   and to know every sort of godlessness.
However many did this for money
have brought punishment upon themselves, but,
since Zeus truly has my reverence still,
know this well, and I will say an oath before you:
315   unless you find the culprit of this tomb
and bring him before these eyes of mine,
Death alone will not protect you:
you'll all be hanged alive to demonstrate
your insolent crime, so the rest of your lives
320   you may steal, knowing once and for all
what sort of reward it brings, and learn that
we must not love all profit equally.
For you should know that more men suffer
from shameful gains than are saved by them.

GUARD:

325   May I say something, or should I just turn and go?

CREON:

You have annoyed me just by saying that!

GUARD:

Does it sting in the ears or in your soul?

CREON:

Why do you care where my pain is located?

GUARD:

The doer troubles your mind, I your ears.

CREON:

330   Oh, it is clear you were born a babbler.

GUARD:

Regardless, I would never do the deed.

CREON:

> You have, and you have sold your soul for cash.

GUARD:

> Alas!
> It's terrible when the one who judges judges wrong.

CREON:

335
> Quibble now about judgments; but if you
> don't show me who did this, you will affirm
> that foul profits reap terrible rewards.

> *Exit* CREON *into the palace.*

GUARD:

> Well, I hope we do find him! But whether
> he's taken or not—for chance controls that—

340
> there's no way you'll see me coming back here.
> Even now beyond my hope and thought I've
> been saved and owe the gods some gratitude.

> *Exit* GUARD *offstage.*

CHORUS:[17]

Str. 1

> This world has many wonders,
> but nothing is more wondrous than humanity.

345
> It crosses even the grey sea
> with a stormy south wind,
> passing under churning waves in open water;
> and the oldest of the gods,
> immortal, inexhaustible Earth,

350
> it wears away.
> With ploughs it winds back and forth,
> year after year,
> turning up the soil with the offspring of horses.[18]

Ant. 1

> He captures and takes

355
> the blithe tribe of birds
> and the races of beasts
> and the salty brood of the sea
> in the coils of woven nets,

[17]*the 1st* stasimon
See *"The Chorus"*
(page 70)

[18]*mules*

a very skillful man. He rules
360   with devices the mountain haunts
of the wild animal
and tames the shaggy-necked horse
with a yoke on its back
and the tireless mountain bull.

Str. 2

365   He taught himself language and wind-like
thought and city-ruling urges,
how to flee the slings of frost
under winter's clear sky
and the arrows of stormy rain, ever-resourceful.
370   Against no possibility
is he at a loss.
For death alone he finds no aid,
but he has devised escape
from impossible diseases.

Ant. 2

375   With clever creativity beyond expectation,
he moves now to evil, now to good.
The one who observes the laws of the land
and justice, our compact with the gods,
is honored in the city, but there is no city
380   for one who participates in what is wrong
for the sake of daring.
Let him not share my hearth,
nor let me share his ideas
who has done these things.

The GUARD returns onstage, leading ANTIGONE.

385   What strange omen now confuses
my sight? How can I deny that
I know this young girl is Antigone?
O poor child of your poor father, Oedipus,
what is this? Have they somehow caught you
390   breaking the king's laws, found you
doing something foolish?

GUARD:

Here she is who did the deed, she's the one
we found burying him—but where is Creon?

Enter CREON *from the palace.*

CHORUS:
> Here he comes from the house, and just in time!

CREON:
395   What is it? What chance makes my coming timely?

GUARD:
> My lord, a mortal should never swear that
> something cannot happen, for hindsight makes
> liars of our plans. Just now I swore I'd
> never come back here, because of those threats
400   you shot at me, but the greatest pleasure
> is the joy you didn't even hope for.
> I came here, despite my oaths to the contrary,
> bringing this girl, who was captured performing
> the rites of burial. This time no lot
405   was shaken; no, this one was my good luck,
> no other's. Now then, my lord, you take her,
> as you wish, and question and sentence her.
> I've justly freed myself from these troubles.

CREON:
> But to bring her? Where did you find her? How?

GUARD:
410   She was burying the man; you know it all.

CREON:
> Do you really mean what you're saying?

GUARD:
> I saw her burying the very corpse you
> forbade. Am I speaking clearly enough?

CREON:
> And how was she seen and caught in the act?

GUARD:

415   This is how it happened: When we came back,
threatened by those terrible things you said,
we brushed off all the dust that was covering
the body, left the clammy thing well and
truly bare. Then, we lay under shelter
420   of the highest hills, fleeing the foul stench;
each man tossing reproaches back and forth,
if any man's attention strayed from this task,
It was that time when the bright circle of
the sun stands in the middle of the sky
425   and the heat burns; suddenly a cyclone
lifted up from the earth a storm of dirt,
a distress of heaven, it fills the plain,
tormenting and ripping apart the trees.
The whole sky was filled. We just closed our eyes
430   and rode out the divine storm. After a while,
it ended, the girl was seen, who was wailing
bitterly like the shrill voice of a bird
who sees her empty nest, stripped of its nurslings.
Thus she screamed, when she saw the uncovered
435   body: She groaned loudly and called down evil
curses on whoever had done the work.
Immediately she gathered dry dust
in her hands and from a jug of fine bronze
lifted up she crowned the corpse with three-fold
440   libations. We saw it and rushed forward,
caught her quickly, completely unperplexed.
We questioned her both about the previous
incident and the current; she stood in
denial of nothing, something for me
445   both sweet and painful, all at once. Nothing
is sweeter than escaping trouble for
yourself, but it's painful to conduct friends
into it. But, for me, everything
takes second place to my own safety.

CREON:

450   You there, staring down at the ground, speak up:
do you affirm or deny doing these things?

ANTIGONE:

> I assert that I did it; I do not deny it.

CREON:

> You, then, may take yourself where you will,
>
> *Exit* GUARD.
>
> rescued from a heavy charge. But, you,
455 tell me briefly, not at length: did you know
> it had been announced not to do this?

ANTIGONE:

> I did. Why would I not know? It was clear.

CREON:

> And yet you dared to overstep these laws?

ANTIGONE:

> Because it wasn't Zeus who pronounced these
460 things to me, nor did Justice, companion
> of the gods below, establish such laws
> for humanity. I would never think
> your pronouncements had such strength that, being
> mortal, they could override the unwritten,
465 ever-lasting prescriptions of the gods,
> for those aren't something recently made, but
> live forever, and no one knows when they
> first appeared. I did not intend to pay
> the penalty to the gods for violating
470 these laws in fear of some man's opinion,
> for I know I will die. How could I not,
> Even if you had not proclaimed it? But
> if I die before my time, I say this
> is an advantage. Anyone who lives
475 a life of sorrow as I do, how could
> they not count it a blessing to die?
> Therefore, there is no pain for me in meeting
> this fate, whereas if I were to endure
> that one born from my mother die unburied,
480 that would cause me pain. As it is, I feel
> nothing. If, however, I seem to you

to have acted foolishly, then perhaps
I owe my foolishness to a fool.

CHORUS:

She's clearly the fierce daughter of a fierce
485   father; she doesn't know to bend with the wind.

CREON:

But know that hard minds fall the hardest, and
that iron, so powerful of itself,
baked to exceeding hardness, you might see
crack and break into pieces. I know that
490   spirited horses are broken with a small bit,
for no one is allowed to think big thoughts,
if he is another man's slave. She showed
herself capable of insolence then,
going beyond the laws put before her.
495   Her second insolence, after she had
done it, was to exult in her deed and
laugh that she had done it. Now I am no man,
but she is a man, if power lies with her
with impunity. No, even if she
500   were closer than my sister's child, closer
than any who share my family's chapel,
she and her sister will not escape the
worst fate, for that girl as well I charge as
equal in plotting this burial. Her, too,
505   bring her here, for I've just seen her inside
in fury, not like someone in full control
of her senses. The heart of one who weaves
wickedness in darkness is usually
convicted beforehand. I, for my part,
510   hate anyone caught in the act who tries
to beautify his crimes thereupon.

ANTIGONE:

Do you want something more than killing me?

CREON:

Nothing more; I have that, and I have it all.

ANTIGONE:

    Then why wait? Nothing you say gives me the
515   slightest pleasure—I pray nothing you say
    ever will—and by nature I offend you.
    And yet, could my fame be more gloriously
    established than by placing my brother
    in a tomb? I think all these people would
520   agree, if fear did not hold their tongues.
    Tyranny is lucky in many ways,
    above all in doing and saying what it will.

CREON:

    You alone of all Cadmus' race think this.

ANTIGONE:

    These think it, too, but hold their tongues for you.

CREON:

525   Aren't you ashamed to think differently from them?

ANTIGONE:

    There's no shame in revering one from the same womb.

CREON:

    And no brother died for the other side?

ANTIGONE:

    A brother by the same mother and father.

CREON:

    Why then this honor insulting to him?

ANTIGONE:

530   The dead man would not agree with you.

CREON:

    If you honor him equally with the wicked.

ANTIGONE:

    This was not his slave who died, but his brother!

19*the name for both
the Underworld
and its king*

CREON:
> Ravaging this land, while he stood in her defense!

ANTIGONE:
> Nevertheless, Hades[19] requires these rites.

CREON:
535   The good don't want to share honors with the bad.

ANTIGONE:
> Who knows what is considered righteous below?

CREON:
> An enemy is not a friend, even when dead.

ANTIGONE:
> I cannot share their hate, only their love.

CREON:
> Then go below, and if you must be loved,
540   love them! No woman will rule while I live.

Enter ISMENE from the palace.

CHORUS:
> But here is Ismene before the doors,
> tears running down her cheeks out of love for her
>> sister.
> A shadow over her flushed brow
> disfigures her face,
545   staining her lovely cheek.

CREON:
> You—like a creeping viper you hid in
> my house, poisoning me. I did not know
> I was nurturing two blights to rebel
> against my throne. Come, tell me—will you also claim
550   a share of this funeral? Do you deny it?

ISMENE:
> I did the deed, if she consents,
> and I will take and bear the charge.

ANTIGONE:
> But Justice will not allow this to you,
> since neither did you want nor did I share it.

ISMENE:
555   But, in your time of trouble, I am not
> ashamed to sail those stormy seas beside you.

ANTIGONE:
> Death and the dead will witness who did the deed;
> I love no friends who are only friends in words.

ISMENE:
> No, sister, do not dishonor me, but let
560   me die with you and honor him who died.

ANTIGONE:
> You may not die with me, nor call yours that
> which you did not touch. My death is enough.

ISMENE:
> Could I desire life when you have left me?

ANTIGONE:
> Ask Creon, since you are his protector.

ISMENE:
565   Why do you grieve me if it does not help yourself?

ANTIGONE:
> If I mock you, I do so with pain.

ISMENE:
> But now—what can I do to help you now?

ANTIGONE:

> Save yourself. I do not grudge you your escape.

ISMENE:

570   Poor girl, am I to have no share in your fate?

ANTIGONE:

> Because you choose to live, and I to die.

ISMENE:

> But not with my arguments left unspoken.

ANTIGONE:

> You seem clever to some, I to others.

ISMENE:

> Then the error is equal for us both.

ANTIGONE:

575   Cheer up. You live, but my soul has been dead
> a long time, that I might serve the dead.

CREON:

> I declare that both these children are fools,
> one just become so, one her whole life.

ISMENE:

> Indeed, my lord, what sense we had does not
580   stand by us in troubles, but goes away.

CREON:

> For you, at least, choosing bad deeds with bad people.

ISMENE:

> What would life be for me alone, without her?

CREON:

> Do not speak of her; she is already gone.

ISMENE:
> You would kill the bride of your own son?

CREON:
585   There are other fields just as fertile.

ISMENE:
> Not with such harmony as he has with her.

CREON:
> I do not want bad wives for my sons.

ISMENE:
> Dearest Haemon, how your father injures you!

CREON:
> You annoy me...and this marriage of yours.

ISMENE:
590   Will you really rob your son of this girl?

CREON:
> Death himself will stop this wedding for me.

ISMENE:
> It is determined, it seems, that she shall die.

CREON:
> For you and me both! Waste no more time, but
> bring them inside now, maids. From now on, they
595   must be women and not wander free, for
> even brave men flee, when they see Death so close.
>   *Exit* ANTIGONE *and* ISMENE *with Servants into the house.*

CHORUS:[20]

                               Str. 1

> Truly blessed are those who have not tasted evil,
> for to them whose house is shaken by the gods,
> no species of madness is left out, creeping over the
600   majority of the family—

[20]*the 2nd* stasimon

like the swell of the salt sea when
the sea's darkness runs upon angry Thracian winds,
it churns up murky sand
from the deep and the storm-swept
605   promontories, beaten by the opposing waves, roar
       with lamentation.

Ant. 1

I see that the old woes of the house of
the Labdacids add to the woes of the dead,
nor does the new generation deliver its race, but one
    of the gods throws them down.
They have no release, for now light has fallen on
610   the last root of the house of Oedipus.
Bloody ashes of the lower gods
now mow her down in turn,
along with the folly of argument and fury of wits.

Str. 2

O Zeus, what human transgression
615   could limit your power?
All-catching Sleep never takes it,
nor the unwearied months of the gods,
but as never-decaying master,
you hold the brilliant radiance of Olympus.
620   The law will prevail,
in time that is, time to come,
as in all time past.
Nothing comes assuredly
to every mortal life—nothing but the rush to ruin.

Ant. 2

625   For indeed wide-ranging hope
is a blessing to many men,
but to many also a trick of light-minded desires.
It comes to one who knows nothing
until he burns his foot
630   walking in hot fire.
Hence the old saying still shows its wisdom:
Sometimes the bad seems good
to one whose wits
God leads to madness.
635   He will last a short time without ruin.

But here is Haemon, the last and youngest
of your children![21] Does he come
in grief for the fate of his
intended bride, the maiden Antigone,
640 in mourning for the bed he was cheated out of?

CREON:

  We will soon know better than predictions.
  Son, can it be that you have heard my final
  vote and come to fight your father for your bride?
  Or am I your friend whatever I do?

HAEMON:

645 Father, I am yours, and as you have me,
  you guide the best course for me to follow.
  No marriage will ever be more important to
  me than justly carrying out your precepts.

CREON:

  And that, child, is how you ought to keep your
650 affections: Stand by your father's ideas
  in all things. This is why a man prays to
  have obedient children in his house:
  that they may take vengeance on their father's
  enemy in bad times and honor his friends
655 as he himself does. But, whoever sires
  useless children—what could you say except
  he has created problems for himself
  and much laughter for his enemies?
  My boy, never give up your wits for a
660 woman because of the pleasure, knowing
  that this darling becomes cold in your arms,
  your wife a wicked concubine in your house.
  And what wound could be worse than a bad friend?
  Therefore, spit her out like an enemy
665 and let her find a husband in Hell.
  Since I caught her, alone of all entire
  people, in open rebellion, I will not
  make myself a liar to the city,
  but kill her. So, let her call on the Zeus

[21]*Creon's older son, Megareus, died to save Thebes from the Argive army. See "Mythological Background" (page 65)*

670   of kinship,22 for if I nurture defiance
        in my relatives, I'd surely have to
        for those outside my clan. Whoever is
        a good man at home is shown to be just
        in the city, too, but whoever goes
675   outside the laws or violates them, or
        thinks to give commands to his superiors,
        this man will not meet praise from me. Rather,
        whomever the city chooses must be
        obeyed in all things—small, just, and the opposite.
680   And this man, I would wager, rules fairly
        and would want to be ruled well, and when marshaled
        under a cloud of spears, he would stand,
        a good and just fighter in the front ranks.
        No evil is worse than disobedience.
685   This one thing destroys cities, turns homes upside
        down, it leads to the rout of allied armies;
        while those who live uprightly are saved by
        obedience. Therefore, rulers must be
        supported, and we must not yield to women.
690   It would be better, if it had to be,
        to fall at a man's hands and not to be called
        worse than a woman.

CHORUS:
        To us, at least, if we are not deceived
        by age, you seem to speak what you say wisely.

HAEMON:
695   Father, the gods endow human beings
        with intelligence, which is the greatest
        of all possessions. I could never—
        I don't know how I could say you don't
        speak correctly, but sometimes another
700   man's opinion is also right. You, however,
        cannot watch everything that people
        say or do or blame, for the common men
        out of fear of your face won't say such words
        as you would not rejoice to hear; but I
705   can hear these things in darkness, how the city

weeps for this girl, says she's the least worthy
of all women to die so badly for
such noble deeds. "She didn't let her brother,
who had fallen in combat, lie unburied,
710   to be devoured by some ravenous
dog or bird. They ought to give her an award!"
So the report spreads in darkness. When you
do well, father, I have no more honored
possession than that, for what prize is greater
715   for children than a father's fame when he's
prospering? Or a son's for his father?
Don't be so stubborn that you say you and
you alone are right. Whoever thinks that
he's the only one who can think or use
720   his tongue or soul, no one else—these men, when
you open them up, are seen to be hollow.
But, for a man to learn, even a wise man,
is nothing shameful, nor to learn to bend
and give way. You see how, in the winter
725   storms, the trees yield that save even their twigs,
but those who oppose it are destroyed root and branch.
Just so the captain who never slackens
his sail once he's stretched it gets his boat turned
and sails the rest with benches upside down.
730   Rather, yield your anger and let yourself change.
Even though I'm young, a good idea
might come from me: It would be best by far
that man be born full of all the knowledge
there is, but, if it usually happens
735   not to turn out that way, to learn from those
who speak well is a good substitute.

CHORUS:
My lord, if someone speaks in season, you should learn,
and you also, for both sides have spoken well.

CREON:
At our age, taught reason by a man so young?

HAEMON:

740   Taught nothing that is not just! If I am young,
      I do not need more time to study what's right.

CREON:

      So, what's right includes revering anarchists?

HAEMON:

      I'd never tell someone to revere the wicked!

CREON:

      Then she has not been taken by this disease?

HAEMON:

745   Her fellow-citizens in Thebes deny it.

CREON:

      The city will tell me how I ought to rule it?

HAEMON:

      Do you hear how rash and young *you* sound?

CREON:

      Should I rule this land for myself or for others?

HAEMON:

      This city does not belong to one man!

CREON:

750   Isn't the city thought to be her ruler's?

HAEMON:

      You'd be a good monarch for a desert.

CREON:

      It seems he's an ally of the woman.

HAEMON:

      If you are a woman! I care only for you!

CREON:
>   Worst of all men, at odds with your own father!

HAEMON:
755   Not when I see you at odds with justice.

CREON:
>   Am I wrong to protect my own empire?

HAEMON:
>   You don't protect it when you trample the
>   honors of the gods!

CREON:
>   Disgusting character!
760   To play the second to a woman!

HAEMON:
>   I would rather yield to her than to evil.

CREON:
>   In any case, this whole speech is for her.

HAEMON:
>   And for you and me and the gods below!

CREON:
>   You cannot marry her while alive.

HAEMON:
765   Then she will die and, dying, destroy another.

CREON:
>   Do you dare to threaten me so boldly?

HAEMON:
>   What threat is it to speak my resolve to you?

CREON:
>   You will regret teaching what you do not know.

HAEMON:
>Were you not my father, I would call you a fool.

CREON:
770   You're the slave of a woman, don't chatter at me.

HAEMON:
>Will you make arguments, but hear no answer?

CREON:
>Really? Then know, by Olympus, that you
>shall not revile me with insults and rejoice!
>Bring the hated thing, so that she may die
775   at once, close by the eyes of her bridegroom.

HAEMON:
>No, not in my sight—never think this can
>happen! She'll not die beside me, and you will
>never lay your eyes upon my face again,
>so rage with any of your friends who can bear it.

>>>>>>>>>>>>>>>>>>>>>>>>>>>>>>>>>>*Exit* HAEMON *offstage.*

CHORUS:
780   My lord, the man has gone quick with anger;
>his mind, at that age, bears pain violently.

CREON:
>Let him go and think superhuman thoughts,
>but he will not save these girls from their doom.

CHORUS:
>Do you intend to kill both of them?

CREON:
785   You're right—not the one who didn't touch him.

CHORUS:
>How do you intend to kill the other?

CREON:

I shall take her to a place completely
devoid of human life and hide her, living,
in a rocky cavern. I'll put in with her
790   as much food as will ward off a curse, so that
our city will escape all pollution.[23]
There she can pray to Hades, the only god
she worships, and perhaps she will find a way
not to die—or learn, though too late for her,
795   that it is excessive work to love the dead.

CHORUS:[24]

                                         Str. 1

Love, unconquered in battle,
Love, who attacks wealth,
who sleeps on a young girl's soft cheek
and wanders beyond the sea and in the wilderness:
800   There is no escape from you for immortals
or men who live but for a day;
he who has you is mad.

                                         Ant 1

You guide even just men's minds
towards injustice, to their destruction.
805   You have even shaken up this kin strife,
through her glances, clear desire of the bride
is victorious, Love the coadjutor
in the great laws of old, for
Aphrodite, the irresistible goddess, is laughing.

Enter ANTIGONE *from the palace, led by* GUARDS.

810   But now I myself am also carried
beyond the laws when I see this.
I can no longer hold back the streams of tears,
when I see Antigone heading for
the bridal chamber where all must sleep.

ANTIGONE:[25]

                                         Str. 2

815   See me, O citizens of my ancestral land,

[23]*If Antigone starves to death, she will not technically have been murdered, according to Greek thought, and, therefore, there will be no pollution for her slayer.* See pollution *in Glossary.*

[24]*the 3rd stasimon*

[25]*At this point, the stasimon becomes a kommos.* See "The Chorus" *(page 70)*

treading the final path,
gazing on the final light of the sun,
never again! But Death, the groom
of all, leads me alive

820   to the promontory of
Acheron;[26] I have no share
of marriage hymns, nor will any
hymn me for my wedding
anyhow, but I shall be the bride of Death.

CHORUS:

825   Therefore, you will go famous and
honored into those depths of the dead.
Not stricken by wasting disease
nor taking the wages of the sword,
but, alone of mortals, you will go,

830   the ruler of yourself, down to Hades.

ANTIGONE:

Ant. 2

I have heard that most sorrowfully did
our Phrygian guest die, the daughter of Tantalus, [27]
on the Sipylan cliff, how, like a vine of ivy,
the petrifying process overwhelmed her,

835   and the rain never leaves her,
languishing there, so men say,
nor does the snow ever leave her,
and beneath her tearful lids
she wets the ridges with her tears;

840   now my destiny sends me to a rest most like hers.

CHORUS:

But she was a goddess and born of gods,
while we are mortals, of mortal race!
Still, it will be to your great fame,
as you die to share the lot of the god-like

845   while you live and, later, when you die.[28]

[26]*a river in the Underworld*

[27]*Niobe, a famous mythological figure, was punished for boasting about her children; see "Niobe" in Glossary. Niobe is called the "Phrygian guest" because she was brought from Phrygia in Asia Minor to marry a Theban.*

[28]*The Chorus is not insulting Antigone, though she thinks this is the case. The Chorus merely reminds Antigone that she is mortal, because it is always bad in Greek thought to compare oneself to a god.*

ANTIGONE:

Oh! I am mocked!
By our fathers' gods, why
do you outrage me, not yet departed,
but still in the light?
850 O city, O rich gentlemen of the city,
hail, springs of Dirce
and grove of many-charioted Thebes,
I'll yet have you as my witness,
how I have no friends to mourn me, by what laws
855 I go to the heaped-up prison
of my unheard of tomb.
Oh, my poor lot, who have no home
among mortals or corpses,
neither the living or the dead!

CHORUS:

860 You went forward far too boldly
and crashed into the lofty
pedestal of Justice, my child.
You are paying for your father's crime.

ANTIGONE:

Ant. 3

You have touched the most
865 painful of my cares,
the thrice-repeated doom of my father
and this whole fate of ours,
the famous Labdacids.
Oh, the sins of my mother's bed
870 and my ill-fated mother's
self-creating intercourse with my father!
From such as these I was born miserable!
I am going to live with them,
accursed, unwed.
875 Oh, my brother, you struck
an unlucky marriage,[29]
and dying you killed me, though I still lived.

[29]*a reference to Polynices' betrothal to the princess of Argos, because of which her father allowed Polynices to lead the Argive army against Thebes*

CHORUS:

> Reverence is a mark of character,
> but power, for a man who has it,
> 880   does not tolerate offenses against itself.
> Your self-guiding anger destroyed you.

ANTIGONE:

Epode

> Unwept, friendless, with no marriage hymn,
> unfortunate, I am taken
> down the prepared road.
> 885   It is no longer right for unhappy me
> to see this holy eye of light,[30]
> but no friend groans
> over my unwept fate.

CREON:

> Don't you know that songs and lament before
> 890   death would never stop, if they did any good?
> Take her away at once, and shut her in
> her walled-up tomb, as I have said. Then leave
> her there alone, where she must either die
> or be entombed alive in such a house,
> 895   for we have no guilt in this maiden's case...
> Regardless, she'll lose her home in the world above.

ANTIGONE:

> O tomb, O bridal bower, o underground
> home everlasting, whither I journey
> to my own people, whose great number—
> 900   so many destroyed—Persephone[31] has
> received among the dead. To these I go down—
> the last of them all and worst by far,
> before my allowance of life is spent.
> Nevertheless, as I go, I nurture
> 905   the hope that I will come dear to my father,
> dear to you, mother, and dear to you, my own
> dear brother. When you died, with my own hands
> I washed and adorned your bodies, and I poured
> libations at your tombs. But now, Polynices,

[30]*the sun*

[31]*wife of Hades and queen of the Underworld*

910 after burying your body, I reap
rewards like these. Still, I honored you well
in the eyes of the wise. No, if somehow
children whose mother I was or my husband
had died, I would not have undertaken
915 this labor in defiance of the citizens.
Shall I tell you the code I follow?
I could get another husband when mine died,
and a child from another man, if I
lost one from him, but since my mother and
920 father[32] both lie in Hell, there is no field
where I could grow another brother.
With this as my law, I honor you above
all others; to Creon I seemed to have
made a mistake and to have done something
925 terrible, my brother. Now he holds me
thus in his hand and leads me, without a
wedding, no bridal hymn, I have no share
of marriage or raising children, but,
as I am, bereft of friends and unlucky,
930 I am going alive into depths of the dead.
Which of the gods' laws have I transgressed?
Why should I still look to the gods in my
unhappiness? What ally can I call?
In my case, by being pious, I have
935 won for myself the rewards of impiety.
But, if these men have sinned, may they not suffer
more evils than they unjustly inflict on me.

CHORUS:
The same violent winds
still rage in her soul.

CREON:
940 Therefore her guards will
suffer for their slowness.

ANTIGONE:
Alas, this word brings closer
my death.

[32]*i.e., Oedipus and Jocasta*

CREON:

I'd be a liar to hearten you,
to say it's not certain.

ANTIGONE:

945   O ancestral town of Thebes
and primeval gods,
I am led away indeed,
no longer merely waiting.

[33]the 4th stasimon

CHORUS:[33]

Str. 1

Danae also dared to exchange
950   the light of day for walls of bronze;[34]
hidden away in a tomb-like
bedroom she was guarded.
Yet, her race was honorable,
O child, my child,
955   and she was the storehouse
of the golden-flowing seed of Zeus.
The power of fate is something terrible.
It cannot be escaped—not with wealth or by war,
not with a tower or a sea-lashed black ship.

Ant. 1

960   The son of Dryas,[35] quick to anger,
the king of Edonia, was yoked by stinging angers,
confined by the will of
Dionysus in a rocky prison.
Thus the flowering, terrible fury of his
965   frenzy dripped away. He learned
to know the god in stinging tongues,
whom he had provoked in his madness.
for he was stopping the races
of women and the Bacchic fire,[36]
970   he irritated the muses who love flutes.

Str. 2

Beside the sea's twin rocks, the Symplegades,[37]
the promontories of the Bosporus,
lies the Thracian Salmydessus,
where the city's neighbor Ares[38]

[34]a mortal woman beloved of Zeus; See Danae in Glossary

[35]Lycurgus, a Thracian king, who denied the godhood of Dionysus and was killed by that god as a result; See Glossary

[36]Dionysus was accompanied by throngs of ecstatic women called Maenads or Bacchants; See Maenads in Glossary

[37]at the straits at the entrance of the Black Sea

[38]Since a god is considered to reside where he has a temple, a city next to that temple would be the god's neighbor.

975   watched the accursed wound dealt
    the two sons of Phineus
    by his fierce wife,[39]
    who blinded their avenging eyes,
    smitten by her bloody hands
980   and the point of her needle.

Ant. 2

    Wasting away unhappily, they mourned
    their unhappy fate and their bastard
    birth from their mother,
    but her seed stretched back to the
985   ancient house of Erechtheus;[40]
    in faraway caves,
    her father nourished her in his hurricanes,
    Boreas, swift as horses over the plains,
    child of the gods. Yet against her, too,
990   the long-loved Fates pressed hard, my child.

Enter TIRESIAS *from offstage.*

TIRESIAS:
    Lords of Thebes, with two watching from one,
    we have come treading our common road,
    for the road for the blind is from the guide.

CREON:
    What news do you have, old Tiresias?

TIRESIAS:
995   I shall teach you, and you—trust the seer.

CREON:
    It is not my custom to disagree with you.

TIRESIAS:
    And thus you have captained this city correctly.

CREON:
    I will testify that you have helped me.

[39]*Idaia, the second wife of King Phineus; See* Idaia *in Glossary*

[40]*legendary first king of Athens*

TIRESIAS:
> Think now that you have walked onto a razor's edge.

CREON:
1000
> What is it? How I shudder at your words!

TIRESIAS:
> You will know when you hear the omens of
> my craft; for sitting on my ancient chair
> of bird-watching,[41] where in the past all the birds
> have gathered for me, I heard a strange new sound—
1005
> birds, screaming with evil, barbaric frenzy;
> and I knew that they were tearing at one
> another with bloody talons, for the rush
> of wings was clear. In fear, I went at once
> to test the burnt sacrifices on the
1010
> blazing altars, but no fire was burning
> on the victims. Rather, upon the embers,
> a dripping ooze trickled from the thigh pieces;[42]
> it smoked and sputtered, and the bile was scattered
> in the air, and the bones lay bare of the fat
1015
> that had covered them. Thus the omens failed,
> there were no signs, as I learned from this boy,
> for he is my guide, as I am to others.
> The city is sick because of your counsel,
> for our altars and all our hearths are defiled
1020
> by birds and dogs with carrion from the corpse
> of the unlucky son of Oedipus.
> For this reason the gods will not accept
> our sacrifices, prayers, and burnt thigh-bones,
> nor do the birds shriek forth clear-signaling cries,
1025
> gorged with a slain man's blood and fat. Therefore,
> think on these things, my child; for every
> human being makes mistakes, but when he has
> made a mistake, that man is no longer
> foolish and unhappy who remedies
1030
> the evil into which he has fallen
> and is not stubborn. Obstinacy brings
> the charge of stupidity. Yield to the dead,
> don't kick a fallen man! What prowess does

[41]*watching the sky for the movement of birds was an important part of Greek prophecy; See* Birds *in Glossary*

[42]*See* Sacrifice *in the Glossary.*

it take to kill one already dead?
1035 My counsel is good, and so is my advice.
To learn from good advice is sweetest, if
the advisor speaks to your advantage.

CREON:
Go ahead, old man; all of you can shoot
your arrows at me like archers at targets.
1040 I am not even left untouched by the seers!
By your kind I was bought and sold and carried
home a long time ago. Make your profit,
purchase electrum[43] from Sardis, if you wish,
and gold from India; but you will not
1045 place him in a tomb, not even if Zeus'
own eagles[44] want to snatch up the carrion
and take it to the very throne of Heaven!
I will not allow him to be buried
out of fear of this pollution, for I
1050 know well that no human is strong enough
to pollute the gods.[45] But, the cleverest
of mortals, old Tiresias, fall with shameful
crash, when they decorate shameful words
for the sake of profit.

TIRESIAS:
1055 Foo.
Does any man know, does any consider…

CREON:
What thing? What great aphorism will you speak?

TIRESIAS:
…how much prudence is the greatest of possessions?

CREON:
(*sarcastically*)
As much as stupidity is the worst hurt?

TIRESIAS:
1060 You certainly seem full of this disease.

[43] *a valuable alloy of gold and silver, closely associated with the Lydian capital of Sardis*

[44] *The eagle was the bird of Zeus.*

[45] *an idea contrary to traditional Greek piety, but in vogue with 5th-century Athenian humanism and rational thinking*

CREON:

I don't want to return the seer's insult.

TIRESIAS:

Yet you do when you say I prophesy lies.

CREON:

The race of seers have always loved money.

TIRESIAS:

And tyrants have always loved cheated profits.

CREON:

1065   Do you realize you speak these lies to your king?

TIRESIAS:

I do, for your city is safe because of me.

CREON:

You're a clever seer, but love injustice.

TIRESIAS:

You will make me say the secret of my knowledge.

CREON:

Do you think I say this for your profit?

TIRESIAS:

1070   Do I seem to do this as far as you're concerned?

CREON:

Know that you'll not barter with my mind.

TIRESIAS:

And you—know well that before the sun has
run a few laps more, you will give one from
your loins, a corpse for corpses, in exchange
1075   for those you have sent from above the earth
to below it, the living soul you have lodged
dishonorably in a tomb, and the

unhappy, unburied, unholy corpse
you hold back from the gods below. You have
1080 no share in this, nor do the gods below,
but this violence comes from you. For these things,
however, the destroying avengers
of Hell and the Furies[46] of the gods are
lying wait for you, that you may be taken
1085 in these same evils. Consider also
if I say these things as a hired accuser,
for a short time will reveal the wailing
of men and women in your house.
All the cities are stirred by hatred, whose
1090 mangled children took their only burial
from dogs and beasts—or some winged bird, bearing
an unholy stench into his native city.[47]
Since you hurt me, like an archer I have left
these words like unswerving arrows of the heart
1095 against your spirit, whose sting you will not escape.
Take me home, boy, so that this man may vent
his anger against younger men and learn
to keep his tongue quieter and fill his mind
with more elevated thoughts than he has now.

Exit TIRESIAS *and Attendant offstage.*

CHORUS:
1100 My lord, this man has gone after prophesying
terrible things, and we know that since I took
this white hair in place of black, he has
never spoken falsely to this city.

CREON:
I know, and I, too, am shaking in my heart,
1105 for to yield is a terrible thing, but it is
just as terrible to give up my anger.

CHORUS:
You must take good advice, child of Menoeceus.

CREON:
What should I do? Tell me, and I will obey.

[46]*ancient and terrible goddesses who avenged crimes committed against kin*

[47]*This indicates that all the slain Argive, not just Polynices, have been denied burial.*

CHORUS:

1110   Go and release the maiden from her rocky
home and make a tomb for the unburied man.

CREON:

You advise this? You think I should yield?

CHORUS:

As soon as possible, my lord, for swift-footed
Divine Vengeance cuts down bad ideas.

CREON:

1115   Alas, it is hard, but I give up what my heart
wished to do. One should not fight necessity.

CHORUS:

Go now and do it, do not leave it to others.

CREON:

I'll go just as I am! Come, come, servants,
those here and those away—grab axes and
rush to that point over there. I myself,
1120   since my judgment has turned and seen better ways,
I bound her and I will go and release her,
for I fear that it is best to keep
the established laws as long as one lives.

CHORUS:[48]

Str. 1

Many-named one,[49] glory
1125   of the Cadmeian bride,[50]
offspring of loud-thundering
Zeus, you who protect famous
Italy, who are lord of
welcoming Eleusis[51]
1130   in the shelter of Demeter, O Bacchus,
inhabitant of Thebes, mother-city
of the Bacchants, by the flowing
stream of Ismenus, where the
dragon's teeth were sown.

[48]Instead of a 5th stasimon, the poet has written here a hyporchema, or dance-song; the chorus is expecting a happy ending.

[49]Dionysus was also known as Bacchus, Iacchus, and Evius, among other names. This ode, which anticipates that Creon will remedy the situation and save the day, is a hymn to Dionysus. It emphasizes the universality of his power and, accordingly, lists many places where he is worshipped.

[50]Semele, the Theban princess who was mother of Dionysus

[51]Dionysus, along with Demeter and Persephone, was worshipped in the Eleusinian mysteries; See Glossary

Ant. 1

1135   The flashing smoke
has seen you
over the double-crested
rock, where Corycian nymphs
go as your Bacchants
1140   by Castalia's stream.
The ivy-covered slopes
of Nysa's mountains and
the green edge, rich in grapes, send you,
visiting the streets of Thebes,
1145   while mortal tongues cry "Evoe!"[52]

Str. 2

You honor this city
above all others
with your thunder-smitten mother,[53]
but now, as the city and all her
1150   people are held by the violence of disease,
come with cleansing fast over
the cliff of Parnassus[54] or the lamenting crossing. [55]

Ant. 2

Hail, dancing-master of the stars,
breathing fire, overseer
1155   of the voices of the night,
child of Zeus, appear,
lord, together with your attendant
Nymphs, who in their madness
dance through the night with you, Iacchus, giver of gifts.

Enter the MESSENGER *from offstage.*

MESSENGER:

1160   Dwellers of the house of Cadmus and Amphion,[56]
there is no sort of human existence
I would ever praise or reproach as static.
Chance sets us up and chance knocks us down,
     good luck
and bad luck, always, and there is no seer
1165   who can tell a man what is destined for him.
Creon was always enviable, I thought,

[52]*the ritual cry in honor of Dionysus, uttered by his ecstatic worshippers*

[53]*Semele; See Glossary*

[54]*the mountain at Delphi, which Dionysus shared with Apollo*

[55]*the strait between Boeotia, the region of Thebes, and the island of Euboea*

[56]*Niobe's husband who built the wall around Thebes*

who saved this land of Cadmus from her foes;
and after taking sole rule of the country,
he ruled, flourishing with a good crop of sons.
1170   And now he has lost it all, for when joy
betrays a man, I count him not as living,
but consider him an animated corpse.
Fill your home with riches, if you wish,
and live with a tyrant's bearing, but if you
1175   lose the joy of these things, I would not buy
them from a man for the shadow of smoke
in exchange for real pleasure.

CHORUS:
What new grief of our kings do you bring us?

MESSENGER:
They are dead, but the living are worthy of death.

CHORUS:
1180   And who slew them? Who has fallen? Tell us!

MESSENGER:
Haemon is lost. His blood was spilled by a
familiar hand.

CHORUS:
By his father's or his own hand?

MESSENGER:
Himself, angry with his father for the murder.

CHORUS:
1185   O seer, how correct your prophecy turned out!

MESSENGER:
With things like this, consider the rest besides.

Enter EURYDICE *from the palace.*

CHORUS:
>And now I see poor Eurydice here,
>Creon's wife. She comes from the house in
>mourning for her son, or perhaps by chance.

EURYDICE:
1190
>Citizens, I heard your words, as I was
>coming to the doors, so that I could go
>and pray before the goddess Athena.
>And just as I was opening the door,
>the sound of my family's misfortune
1195
>struck my ears, and I fell back, afraid,
>against my maids, and lost my senses.
>Still, tell the story again, whatever
>it is, for I am already used to trouble.

MESSENGER:
>Dear mistress, I shall say what I witnessed,
1200
>and I shall leave out not one word of the truth.
>Why should I soothe you with words that will later
>reveal me a liar? The truth is always right.
>I was following your husband as a guide
>into the farthest part of the plain, where
1205
>the unpitied corpse of Polynices,
>torn by dogs, still lay. There, asking the goddess
>of the crossroads[57] and Pluto[58] to hold back
>their righteous anger and bathing his body
>as custom demands, we gathered what was left
1210
>of him in newly-plucked branches, and, heaping
>a high tomb of his native soil, we headed
>to the stone-paved chamber of the bride of Death.
>Someone heard the shrill voice of mourning
>near the unhallowed chamber and pointed it
1215
>out to our master Creon. Who had uttered
>the tortured cry was still unknown to him
>creeping still closer, but he groaned and sadly
>said, "Am I the prophet of my own doom?
>Was it an unlucky road I traveled here?
1220
>The voice of my child greets me…servants, quick,
>go closer! Stand by the tomb and, at the gap

[57]*Hecate, a witch-goddess associated with death*

[58]*another name for the god of the Underworld*

in the rocks, find out if I recognize
the voice of Haemon or if the gods deceive me!"
At the command of our despairing master,
1225　we did observe; and in the last part of
the tomb, we saw her hanged by the neck, fastened
by a noose of fine linen, and him wrapped
around her, clinging to her around the waist,
bewailing the destruction of his lost bride
1230　and the deeds of his father and his unhappy
marriage bed. When the king saw them, he groaned
dreadfully and went inside towards the pair,
calling in lament, "Daring boy, what is
this thing you've done? What were you thinking?
1235　What misfortune has destroyed your mind?
Come out, child; as a suppliant, I beg you."
The boy glared at him wildly, spat in his face
and answered nothing, but drew his sword.
　　　　He missed
his father, as he leapt away. Then, the poor boy,
1240　in his anger at himself, guided the sword,
leaned on it and thrust it into his ribs
up the hilt; and while he still had sense,
he pulled the maiden into his dying embrace.
With his dying breath he sent a river
1245　of crimson blood dripping down her white cheek.
There they lay, corpse on corpse, and, poor thing,
he got his wedding rites in the house of Death,
showing to humanity by how much
foolishness is the greatest evil for a man.

Exit EURYDICE *into the palace.*

CHORUS:
1250　What do you make of that? The lady has fled,
before she could say a word, good or bad.

MESSENGER:
I, too, am astonished, but I am fed
by hopes that she does not think it right to mourn
her son's fate in front of the city,
1255　but will set her maids to mourn their household's

grief under their own roof. She is not so
foolish that she would do something rash.

CHORUS:
> I don't know: To me, excessive silence
> seems to bode as ill as too much shouting.

MESSENGER:
1260   Then I will go and find out, lest she conceal
> something hidden in her angry heart as
> she goes inside the house. You are right:
> There is also grief in too much silence.

                  Exit MESSENGER *into the palace.*

CHORUS:
> And now the king himself approaches, bearing
1265   in his arms a memorial to,
> if it is right to say it, no foreign
> madness, but showing his own mistakes.

Enter CREON *from offstage.*

CREON:[59]

                                    Str. 1

> Oh!
> Mistakes from thoughtless thoughts,
1270   stubborn and deadly!
> O men who have seen
> kin slaying and dying,
> alas, for the misfortune of my plans!
> Oh, my son—forever young by this untimely death,
1275   alas, alas!
> You died, you were sent away
> by my foolish counsels, not your own.

CHORUS:
> I think you have seen justice too late.

CREON:
> Alas!

[59]kommos

1280   I have learned pathetically,
        but then—oh, then some god was angry and hit
            me hard
        in the head and shook me on fierce roads,
        alas, overturned and trampled my happiness.
        Oh, the ill-labored labors of mortals!

Enter 2nd MESSENGER *from the palace.*

2nd MESSENGER:
1285   O master, you have enough evils already,
        the ones you carry now in your arms,
        and those in the house you will see soon.

CREON:
        What is left more evil than these evils?

2nd MESSENGER:
        Your wife is dead, the mother of this very corpse,
1290   poor creature, just now by recent strokes.

CREON:
                                                           Ant. 1
        Oh!
        Oh, haven of Death, so hard to appease,
        why, oh why do you ruin me?
        O you who have announced these
1295   grievous pronouncements to me, what word do
            you utter?
        Oh, oh! You have slain again a man already
            destroyed!
        What do you say, boy? Why do you tell me this news,
        alas, alas,
        this seal upon my ruin,
1300   to add on my wife's fate?

CHORUS:
        It is here to see, no longer hidden within.

The body of EURYDICE *is rolled out upon the* ekkyklema. 60

CREON:

    Alas!

    Now I see this second, other evil.

    What, oh what lot still awaits me?

1305   I have just held my child in my arms,

    poor thing, and here is another corpse before me.

    Alas for the poor mother, alas for the child.

2nd MESSENGER:

    Stung by passion, at the altar she loosed

    her darkening eyes, lamenting first the

1310   famous death of Megareus, who died before,

    and then of this one, and last she called down

    evil fortune on you, the child-slayer.

CREON:

Str. 2

    Alas, alas!

    I am shaken with fear. Will no one strike

1315   me the mortal blow with a double-edged sword?

    I am a wretch, alas,

    and I am made whole by wretchedness.

2nd MESSENGER:

    Yes, and you are responsible for these deaths

    and hers whose corpse you see before you.

CREON:

1320   How did she come to die so bloodily?

2nd MESSENGER:

    She struck herself in the heart with her own hand,

    when she learned of the sad fate of her boy.

CREON:

    Woe is me, these things will never fall

    on another person so as to exonerate me,

1325   for I killed you, O unhappy

    I, I claim it truly. Servants,

    take me away right now, take me out of the way.

    I don't exist any more; I'm no one.

CHORUS:

> You offer good advice, if there is any good
1330
> in suffering. The quickest solution
> is best when troubles are in your way.

CREON:

Ant. 2

> Go, go—
> let it appear, that most beautiful of all fates,
> the one bringing me my last day,
1335
> the very best fate! Go, go—
> so that I may never look upon another day!

CHORUS:

> What will be will be. We must act on what lies
> before us. The future is the gods' concern.

CREON:

> That's all I was saying, my entire prayer.

CHORUS:

1340
> Don't pray any more; it is not for mortals
> to escape our destined misfortune.

CREON:

> Let this rash man be led out of the way,
> who, my child, unwillingly slew you,
> and this woman, you, too—alas! I have
1345
> no where to turn to, nothing to lean on,
> for everything goes cross in my hands,
> and a difficult fate falls on my head.

> > *Exit* CREON, *led by Attendants, into the palace.*

CHORUS:

> Knowledge truly is by far the most important part
> of happiness, but one must neglect nothing
1350
> that the gods demand.
> Great words of the over-proud
> balanced by great falls
> taught us knowledge in our old age.

Mythological Background

SINCE TRAGEDIES WERE BASED on widely-known myths or famous historical events, the audience would know the characters and outline of the story they were about to see. Most surprises, therefore, did not come from the plot, although playwrights could introduce innovations into the story. In seeing a play about Antigone, the audience would already know that this story came from the cycle of myths about the city of Thebes, one of Athens' rivals in the 5th century BCE. The story is set a few generations before the Trojan War, Laius, the king of Thebes, received a prophecy that his son would kill him. To avoid this outcome, when a child was born to

Oedipus

Laius and his queen, Jocasta, he had the baby exposed on Mount Cithaeron, at the edge of his kingdom. He nailed the child's feet together as an extra precaution (a common way to get rid of unwanted infants throughout the historical period). Unfortunately for Laius, the baby survived and was raised as a prince of the city of Corinth with the name Oedipus, which means "swollen foot" in Greek.

Many years later, Oedipus, not knowing his true birth, met Laius on the road. Without either man knowing the identity of the other, an argument arose, and Oedipus unknowingly killed his father. Around that same time, Thebes was being terrorized by the Sphinx, a monster with the head of a woman, body of a lion, and wings of an eagle. The Sphinx was particularly famous for asking everyone who encountered her a riddle; when they could not answer it, she devoured them. This was her riddle: "What walks on four legs in the morning, two legs in the afternoon, and three legs in the evening?" The person to solve this riddle was Oedipus, the answer being 'man' (who crawls as a baby, walks on two legs as an adult, but leans on a cane in his old age). Her riddle solved, the Sphinx threw herself from a cliff, and Oedipus was crowned king of Thebes and married the recently widowed queen, his own mother, Jocasta. Years passed before the gods

Oedipus and the sphinx

brought the incest to light, after which Jocasta committed suicide, and Oedipus blinded himself, living the rest of his life as a homeless wanderer.

Oedipus and Jocasta had several children together, but when his sons disobeyed

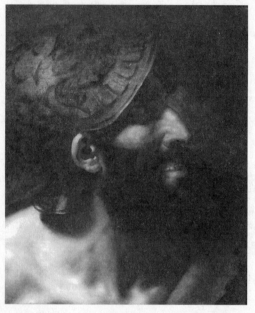

Capaneus, leader of The Seven against Thebes.

him, Oedipus cursed them, thus continuing the family's wretched destiny. Oedipus then died either at Thebes or in exile; the myths are inconsistent. Soon, a quarrel arose between Oedipus' sons, Eteocles and Polynices. The latter, although older, was exiled and journeyed to the powerful city of Argos, where he won the favor of the Argive king. The king betrothed his daughter to Polynices, who returned to Thebes at the head of an Argive army. The panic-stricken city was defended by Eteocles and six others, who met Polynices and six heroes (the famous "Seven Against Thebes," subject of a play by Aeschylus) from other areas of Greece at each of the city's seven gates. The Thebans were victorious and the Argive army left the city. Polynices and Eteocles, however, killed each other simultaneously, leaving the kingship to Jocasta's brother Creon. Creon also took custody of Oedipus' remaining children, two young daughters named Antigone and Ismene.

The Importance of Burial in Greek Religion

FOR THE MOST PART, the Greeks did not believe in a different afterlife for the good or bad (i.e., no heaven or hell). In their view, the afterlife was almost universally grim; the important detail for the dead was whether they were buried or unburied. Those who did not receive proper funeral rites were doomed to wander by the river Styx, the entrance to the Underworld, for eternity; their souls could never be at rest. Thus, denying burial to a corpse not only insulted the body, but also damned its soul for all time.

The buried were granted access to Hades, the name of both the Underworld and its king. In order for the dead to gain access, a complicated ritual had to be performed. There were few 'professional' undertakers, so a man's funeral fell to his family, especially to the women. They prepared the body for cremation, oversaw the collection of the bones and ashes and burial of the urn, provided the tomb with liquid

The River Styx

offerings (libations), and led the mourning, a loud and violent process in which women tore their cheeks with their fingernails, ripped out their hair, and poured dirt over their heads and clothing.

Mourning the dead was one of the few things women were allowed to do in ancient Greece, especially Athens. Women of well-born families were expected to stay at home in specially designated women's quarters at all times except during certain religions festivals. Marriages were arranged by a girl's father or guardian. Women were not true citizens of the democracy and could not speak or vote in the assembly. They were not even allowed to speak in court, a basic right for men.

Burying and mourning their dead relatives gave women an opportunity to do something important for their families. It brought women to the fore and gave them a role to play. Therefore, when Creon forbids the burial of Polynices, he is denying Antigone the opportunity to perform one of the most significant duties that Greek society allowed for women. Thus, he is attacking her identity, and that is a part of the reason she opposes his orders.

Greek Tragedy: An Overview

Tragedy and the City

TRAGEDY IS A PARTICULAR PRODUCT of the Athenian democracy. In the late 6th century BCE, the Athenians drove out the family of tyrants who had ruled the city for decades and established the first government that was close to a democracy in western history. Almost all political offices were chosen by lot, and the assembly of all Athenian citizens voted directly on all important issues. It was during the 5th century that Athens became the most powerful city of Greece. After joining with other Greek cities to repel an invasion by Persia, the largest empire in the world at the time, Athens became an imperial power herself, conquering other Greek cities; eventually, though, the Athenians stretched their power too far and their rule collapsed. Sparta and her allies conquered Athens in 404, and, although the democracy was restored and continued throughout the 4th century, Athens would never regain the glory she had achieved a century earlier.

Fifth-century Athens was almost unparalleled in its cultural achievement, from philosophy and science through architecture and the visual arts. Tragedy was the premiere literary genre of this period, and it is fitting that the apex of the democracy should be symbolized by a genre of poetry that involved the entire body politic. Performed at one of the major festivals of the city, the Great Dionysia, each tragedy was part of a contest. Three playwrights would be chosen by a city official, and each playwright would produce three tragedies and a satyr-play (a kind of farce intended to lighten the mood after the tragedies); all four plays being performed in a single day. The audience consisted of about 15,000 citizens, and the festival itself became a pageant of Athenian power and glory.

We know of many playwrights from this century, but the works of only three survived the end of antiquity and the Middle Ages, in which so much of ancient literature was lost. Fortunately, the three poets we have were universally considered to be the best: Aeschylus, Sophocles, and Euripides. From Sophocles, who won twenty victories (compared to Aeschylus' thirteen and Euripides' four) we have the seven plays chosen by ancient critics as his finest: *Ajax, The Women of Trachis,*

Electra, Philoctetes, and the so-called "Theban plays," *Oedipus Tyrannus, Oedipus at Colonus,* and *Antigone.* These three plays are not a trilogy *per se*; they were not written in order or performed together at one festival. In fact, about forty years separates the first play written, *Antigone,* from the last, *Oedipus at Colonus.* Each play, therefore, should be considered a separate work, and while Sophocles alludes to his earlier work, he pursued different goals and used different methods for each one.

The Genre of Greek Tragedy

Greek legend attributed invention of acting to Thespis, which is why we call actors "thespians." Drama was born when, instead of just narrating events, an actor assumed a character and interacted accordingly with the chorus, who were also now seen as persons specific to the drama. (In *Antigone*, the chorus is made up of the elders of Thebes.) Both actor and chorus performed wearing elaborate costumes and masks. According to the philosopher Aristotle, Sophocles' predecessor Aeschylus added the second actor and Sophocles himself the third. With these three actors playing multiple roles (by changing their masks backstage), a complete story could be acted out, and gradually the role of the chorus diminished. In the plays of Sophocles, the chorus rarely achieves the role of a real character as it so often does, for instance, in the plays of Aeschylus.

The plays followed a fairly strict structure, with a prologue, the entrance of the chorus, and then several episodes separated by choral odes. The dialogue of the plays is written in meter, like the plays of Shakespeare, whereas the choral odes were written in a more complicated meter to which the chorus could sing and dance. The plays also include a *kommos*, in which the main character(s) lament in song with the chorus. The form of Greek tragedy occupies a place somewhere between Shakespeare and opera. It is important for modern readers to remember that they are getting a small portion of what the original audience received, for they are reading a *libretto* without the benefit of music, costumes, or scenery.

Conventions of the Genre

The most important convention of the Greek stage was that all performers wore masks with attached wigs. As such, facial expression, which plays so large a role in modern theater, was not a factor. Additionally, the elaborate costumes worn by the actors and chorus members were often the most striking visual element. Staging was usually limited to a painted background behind the stage. Greek tragedies are all set outside, so the background usually depicted the exterior of the main character's residence (in *Antigone*'s case, the palace of Thebes). Changes of scene are rare in Greek tragedy, and props are kept to a minimum. The action of the drama takes place over a single day. In addition to the chorus and the three actors, mute characters could also appear on stage as needed. In front of the stage proper, which was not raised from the ground as in modern theaters, was a circular area called the *orchestra*, in which the chorus performed its dances. These would have musical accompaniment provided by an *aulos*, a double pipe similar to a modern oboe.

The Chorus

Since Greek tragedy grew out of the performances of lyric poetry sung by large choruses, it is only natural that the chorus should remain a large part of Greek tragedy. Every play's Chorus (usually fourteen men) took on an identity appropriate to the play. For example, in *Antigone*, it is old men of Thebes; in Aeschylus' *Eumenides*, it is the dread goddesses, the Furies.

The word *chorus* in Greek means "dance," and the Chorus' main function was to sing and dance lyric *odes* between dramatic episodes. These odes comment on the action of the preceding episode. An ode (also called a *stasimon*) usually consists of alternating stanzas, the *strophe* and *antistrophe*, which are in the same meter. Since odes are composed in lyric meters (as opposed to chanted iambic trimeters of the dialogue), these stanzas would be very complicated. Additionally, the main character(s) of a play could join the Chorus in a *kommos*, a lyric song sung by both character and Chorus at a point of heightened emotion.

The Chorus was never on stage at the beginning of a play. Instead, after the play's prologue, the Chorus members marched into the *orchestra*, the circular area in front of the stage where they danced. As they marched in, the Chorus members chanted a *parodos* to introduce themselves. The parodos is neither a lyric song nor ordinary dialogue, but is metrically between these modes.

The Chorus could also act as a character; one chorus member would be designated leader and speak lines of dialogue, interacting with the other characters on stage. The Chorus reacts as its character should—in *Antigone*, the Chorus is concerned with both religious and civic obligations; thus, they can see the good and bad sides to both Antigone's and Creon's arguments. The Chorus feels pity for both Antigone and Creon when they suffer, but it is not emotionally involved in the play's outcome the way the individual characters are.

Glossary

Argos – an important city in the Peloponnese (southern part) of Greece; in the 6th century BCE, Argos was one of the greatest cities in Greece. It is often considered the home of the legendary king Agamemnon, who led the Greeks in the Trojan War. By the 5th century BCE, when this play was written, Argos had faded from its leading position. It was still valuable to the Athenians, though, because it was a rival of their principal enemy, Sparta.

Birds – The Greeks thought that the gods communicated to mortals through birds. Different birds indicated different things, as did the actions of those birds. Since Tiresias is blind, he listens to the birds' cries for hints about the future, but Tiresias is an especially powerful seer and could prophesy just as well without birds.

Danae – a mortal woman beloved of Zeus; her father locked her in a room, which Zeus entered by assuming the form of a golden rain. The result of their union was the hero Perseus.

Ekkyklema – One of Athenian theatre's two 'special effects;' the *ekkyklema* was a wheeled platform which could roll out from behind the *scaena* (stage front), from inside the house that served as backdrop of the play. It was usually used to roll out bodies of characters who had died in the house (since violence was almost never shown onstage). For instance, in Aeschylus' *Agamemnon*, Clytemnestra, having murdered her husband Agamemnon in the bath, declares her rule of the city of Argos while the *ekkyklema* rolls out to reveal the bloody corpse of the dead king.

Eleusinian mysteries – one of the most important cults in Greece; Dionysus, along with Demeter and Persephone, was worshipped in these mysteries. Unlike standard Greek religion, the cult promised its believers salvation and paradise after death.

Gods and goddesses – Greek religion was polytheistic; the Greeks worshipped many gods. The most powerful was Zeus, the sky god, who was thought to have taken power when he overthrew his father, Cronus. After Zeus came the other Olympian deities, including Zeus' queen, Hera; his brother, Poseidon; and his children, Athena, Ares, Artemis, and Apollo. There were also other gods, older deities from the reign of Cronus who remained powerful and were considered irrational. Among these were the Furies, dread goddesses who hunted down and drove insane those people who killed blood-relatives.

The most important god in *Antigone* is Zeus, who guards justice from his position as king of heaven. It was thought that Zeus protected Themis, a goddess who was a personification of 'right,' as opposed to 'wrong.' Themis enforced both the keeping of oaths and humans' obligations to each other. Such enforcement ensured the orderly functioning of the universe and was, therefore, very important to Zeus.

Justice – For the Greeks, justice meant doing good to your friends and harm to your enemies. *Antigone* highlights the complications that could arise from acting upon this definition. Creon defines an enemy as anyone who turns against his city, but Antigone sees only family ties as sacred. Hence, they have different views of the fallen Polynices. Each, however, is convinced that his or her own course is just.

Idaia – the second wife of King Phineus of Thrace; she wanted to secure the kingdom for her own sons, so she blinded the sons of Phineus by his first wife, Cleopatra, the daughter of Boreas, the West Wind, and an Athenian princess. It is Cleopatra who is the analogy to Antigone, as was Danae.

Lycurgus – a Thracian king who denied the godhood of Dionysus as that god made his triumphal entry into Greece from the East; Dionysus responded by driving Lycurgus mad. After Lycurgus committed many crimes, he was arrested by his people and shut up in a cave, where he was killed by wild animals.

Maenads – throngs of ecstatic women who accompanied Dionysus—also called Bacchants; Their behavior was considered undesirable by ruling powers in various cities, who suppressed the cult of Dionysus.

Niobe – a queen of Thebes who had 14 children—seven sons and seven daughters; she boasted that she had more children than Leto, a goddess, who had only two. Unfortunately for Niobe, these two children were the powerful deities Apollo and Artemis, both of whom were associated with archery. Using their infallible arrows, Apollo and Artemis slew all of Niobe's children (Apollo killing the boys, Artemis the girls), and Niobe herself fled to a mountain, where she was turned to stone, although she continued to weep. (This phenomenon explained the image of a weeping woman formed by a spring in the porous limestone of the mountain.)

Niobe is frequently alluded to in Greek literature because she is the perfect symbol for the suffering that comes, justly or not, from opposing or slighting authority. She was also the subject of tragedies in her own right, the most famous being that of the great playwright Aeschylus, whose play showed Niobe sitting on the stage, silently weeping, for over half of the drama before she said her first line.

Pollution – The Greek word is *miasma*, which means the pollution that comes from a crime offensive to the gods. Most often associated with a crime like murder or incest that violates natural law as well as human law, the idea could also be extended to cover not burying someone, which has obvious health risks, in addition to religious ones.

Pollution affected both the agent and location of the crime, as well as any person or place harboring the criminal. Proper ritual cleansing (*katharsis*) was necessary to restore both person and place to an acceptable state. Antigone sees her brother's unburied corpse as *miasma*, and so she will do whatever is necessary to perform the proper rituals to end the pollution that keeps her brother from peace in the Underworld. Creon, on the other hand, makes the rather revolutionary statement that men cannot pollute the gods, indicating his more modern 'humanistic' beliefs. Both views could be justified in 5th-century Athenian thought.

Prophecy – In order to understand the will of the gods, the Greeks used many methods of prophecy, which included consulting oracles (holy places in which humans could pose questions and receive answers through the god's chosen interpreter), inspecting the entrails of a sacrificed animal, or watching the motion of birds in the sky. All of this had to be done by a prophet, a specially chosen priest who could interpret such things. Tiresias is probably the most famous prophet in Greek myth, and the Athenian audience would know that whatever he said was true.

Sacrifice – Greek religion, for the most part, did not follow a moral code, but consisted of acts and prayers designed to win the favor of the gods. The ritual slaughter of an animal was considered the best way to do this, although other offerings could also be made, such as pouring a libation (liquid offering) of milk, wine, honey, or placing a gift of flowers or incense beside a statue of a god. Animal sacrifice involved slitting the animal's throat and collecting the blood in a bowl. The animal would then be slaughtered; the meat would be roasted and eaten by the humans performing the festival (generally the only time Greeks ate roasted meat), while the thighbones would be wrapped in fat and burned on the altar as a gift to the gods. The priest would also inspect the entrails of the animal during the slaughter—if anything was amiss (for example, the liver was diseased or missing), it was a sign that the gods had not accepted the sacrifice and something bad was at work.

Semele – another mortal woman beloved of Zeus; mother of Dionysus. Zeus' jealous wife Hera tricked Semele into asking Zeus to see him in his full glory as a god, which overwhelmed her mortal eyes. She burned to death, but Zeus grabbed the unborn Dionysus as she went up in flames.

Thebes – a city of Boeotia, in the northern part of mainland Greece; Thebes was one of the most famous cities in ancient times, and many myths are set there. In the 5th century BCE, Thebes was a rival to Athens.

Vocabulary

accursed – cursed, damned

adorned – ornamented, decorated

affirm – to confirm; to acknowledge

ally – a helper or supporter

alternative – an option or choice

anarchists – people who revolt against laws or the government; rebels

animated – active; alive

aphorism – a wise saying

appease – to satisfy or soothe

assert – to state with force

assuredly – surely, certainly

avenging – seeking revenge

barbaric – savage; hostile

barter – to trade goods or services as a method of payment

base – dishonorable; immoral

benefactor – a supporter or savior

bereft – deprived

bewailing – grieving; expressing sorrow

bile – digestive fluid

blights – plagues; diseases

blithe – carefree; unconcerned

bode – to predict or foretell

brandished – held or waved (an object) in a threatening or showy way

brood – offspring

carcass – a dead body

carrion – decaying flesh

circumstance – formal display; ceremony

coadjutor – a helper or accomplice

concubine – a mistress

consistent – reliable, dependable; unchanging

contentious – belligerent, argumentative

culprit – a person guilty of a crime or wrongdoing

decreed – commanded, ordered

defiled – violated; contaminated

denounce – to condemn or criticize

descending – coming down

deviate – to stray or turn away from the norm

devised – planned, schemed

devoid – empty; lacking

disfigures – makes less attractive; blemishes

dishonorable – disgraceful, shameful

edict – a law or command

embers – hot ashes

endow – to grant or give

entombed – buried; sealed away

enviable – lucky, fortunate

erstwhile – former, previous

excessive – extreme; immoderate

exile – separation from one's country as a form of punishment or by choice

exonerate – to clear of blame or responsibility

expelled – drove or forced out

exult – to show joy or triumph

fatherland – one's home country or native land

flourishing – thriving, growing

foes – enemies

forbade – refused to allow

fratricidal – relating to the act of killing one's brother or sister

girt – encircled; surrounded

gloriously – famously; greatly

godlessness – sinfulness; wickedness

gorged – stuffed, overfilled

grievous – dreadful, terrible

haven – a home or place of safety

hearten – to cheer up or encourage

hearth – home, family warmth

hindsight – understanding something after it has happened

immortal – undying, eternal

impiety – sinfulness; disrespect for someone or something sacred

impunity – freedom from blame or responsibility

inexhaustible – infinite, endless; vast

infamous – well known for something bad

inflict – to cause pain; to force

inhabitant – one who lives in a place; a resident

insolent – rude; disrespectful

insufferably – unbearably, intolerably; offensively

kinsman – a relative

languishing – weakening; wasting away

libations – liquid offerings used in religious rituals
lofty – exalted
marshaled – assembled, gathered
marvel – an amazing sight
mattock – a tool used for digging
monarch – a king
noble – righteous, virtuous
nurslings – babies still being nursed by their mother
oblivion – a state of forgetfulness or ignorance
obstinacy – stubbornness
offenses – crimes, sins
offspring – children, descendants
onslaught – an attack or assault
override – to take priority over
pathetically – sadly; pitifully
pedestal – a column-like stand which supports and elevates an object
per se – [Latin] in and of itself; essentially
petrifying – hardening
pious – religious, devout
pomp – a showy display; a spectacle
ponder – to think
precepts – rules, laws
prevailed – triumphed; dominated
primeval – original; ancient
privy – knowing or sharing in secret knowledge
proclaim – to announce publicly
promontories – high, rocky pieces of land that jut out into the sea
pronouncements – declarations; statements
prophesy – to predict the future
prospering – doing well; achieving success
prowess – superior ability, skill
prudence – good judgment
radiance – a brightness; energy
ravaging – destroying, ruining
ravenous – hungry; greedy
reap – to harvest; to bring in
remedies – makes better; fixes
reproaches – accusations; criticisms
resolve – decision; determination
resourceful – inventive; practical

revered – respected; admired

revile – to insult or abuse

rout – a crushing defeat

seer – one who sees the future; a prophet

sires – fathers, begets children

slackens – loosens, relaxes

slew – killed

smiting – striking; damaging, destroying

static – unchanging, unmoving

stoning – the practice of killing someone by hitting with stones

stricken – afflicted; harmed

strife – trouble; conflict

succumb – to surrender or give in

summoning – sending for; convening

suppliant – person requesting something from a leader

talons – claws

thrice – three times

transgression – a crime or wrongdoing

treading – walking

tyranny – a form of government in which a single ruler holds absolute power

tyrants – cruel and oppressive rulers

unhallowed – unholy; evil

unlamented – not mourned over

unperplexed – not confused; clear-headed

unswerving – straight; direct

uprightly – virtuously, morally

uttered – voiced, expressed

valor – courage, bravery

vengeance – revenge

venture – an endeavor; a task

villainous – wicked

viper – a snake

whither – where

Oedipus and Antigone.
by Antoni Brodowski